AUTUMN WINDOW

poems by

William Marr

forewords by

Glenna Holloway

and

Li-Young Lee

Autumn Window

Library of Congress Catalog Card Number: 95-95217
ISBN: 0-9637547-4-2

1995 •FIRST EDITION
ARBOR HILL PRESS
NAPERVILLE
ILLINOIS

For Jane

Foreword

It's often said of East and West that "never the twain shall meet," but the poetry of William Marr belies that adage. Not only do the twain meet in his voice and his verse, they embrace. A master of lyrical layers along with the beauty and brevity of his Chinese heritage, he enhances his skill with the spontaneity and flavor of his adopted American homeland. His humor, insight and tenderness are universal; his control of such rich ingredients is sure-handed. *AUTUMN WINDOW* is distillation in its purest form: A delightful wine with a rare bouquet.

- Glenna Holloway
past president
Illinois State Poetry Society

Foreword

These poems read to me like notes a lone man might make to himself as reminder to see the world more clearly, transparently. Their subject is, finally, transparency. Each is a window opening onto beauty and fluency. There is every shade of happiness and sadness, anger and peace in this collection. Their effortless renderings of a civilized mind in touch with an often mad world are part of their mystery. Mr. Marr is modern because of the free-verse he employs, but ancient due to the eternal quality of his observations. Ranging from whimsical to disturbing, these poems are lovely. Unassuming and simple on the surface, they suggest a sensibility both light and dark. A very complete collection of a representative man representing.

- Li-Young Lee
Poet, Author of
Rose
The City in Which I Love You
The Winged Seed

Contents

III. IN THE WINDY CITY

IV. DIALOGUE

V. FOUR SEASONS

I.

AT THE WATERFALL

Bird Cage

open
the
cage

let the bird fly

away

and
give
the cage
back
its
freedom

Dandelion

The horizon is so far away
that the dandelion makes its roaming
dream
a relay event

from
    generation
          to
            generation

Sharing an Umbrella

Sharing an umbrella
I suddenly realized the difference
between us

Yet bending over to kiss you
gave me such joy
as you tried to meet me halfway
on tiptoe

A Loose Afternoon

Light-footed
lest I should startle the squirrel
at the foot of a tree
nibbling at a tender piece
of the early spring sun

Still there's the warning cry of a bird

Yet what makes the squirrel climb
to the treetop
is apparently not fear
for in its rushing path through the branches
green buds open up, one after another
to greet its gaiety
in the spring breeze
of April

Last Life

roaming somewhere in the universe
a clang from an anvil
or a hollow resonance from the woods
is yet to reach me
otherwise I might be able to tell you
in my last life
I was a blacksmith
or a woodpecker

a painter, or a flower
if only I could recall
the face of an evening sky
still wet on canvas
or a brilliant dewdrop
precariously rolling
and rolling

a trace of cloud
a whiff of air...

At the Waterfall

Deep in the mountain
there are plenty of caves
where one can sit in solitude
and meditate

Yet I stand here full of joy
looking up at the waterfall
as enlightened thoughts
dart through the air
like thousands
of silvery horses

Mountain

It's still there
for me to
climb

Looming from my childhood
my father's
back

Necktie

Before the mirror
he carefully makes himself
a tight knot

to let the hand
of civilization
drag him
on

Kissing

It makes no difference—
your lips kissing my lips
or my lips kissing yours

What's important
is that we still have something
to say to each other
and try to say it
well

Sometimes You

Sometimes you pull down the curtains
and make your face a tall window
aloof
far from the ground
shutting out the sunshine
shutting out laughter
shutting out all concerned gazes

Though my courting days are long past
all night I wander beneath your window
hoping to catch, in the thick of the curtains
a glimpse of your eyes
like the flickering stars
behind heavy clouds

The Thinker

Holding his chin
thinking
how to
hold the chin
and watch the computer
do
the thinking

Reading

As soon as he opens the book
words lead the way
and sentences follow
all disappear in a hurry

Only the best-selling title
and the hotly talked-about name
of the author
remain

What a great book

Story

The dog has its eyes closed
but the old man knows it's listening

Its warm back is moving
ever closer

A Cloudy Day

Even with a bellyful of sorrow
he is unable to cry

The listless, unopened umbrella
becomes increasingly
a burden

In Memory of

On the moonless sky
each star
is a grain of sand
in my shoes of memory
to remind me
of your existence

A Post-It Note

I've put some
poems
in the icebox

they'll be cold
and sweet
when you get home

Ears

Tuned to loud noises
ears are shocked
by a deafening
sudden

silence

Morning Song

With dewdrops to refresh
their throats
the birds know
sooner or later
the worms will stick out
their sleepy heads

Daybreak

I don't care what the weatherman says
it's going to be a fine day

Already I can see far and near
birdcalls rise
and prick the dark sky
making slits
to let light in

Tree

I feel
something wheeling
in my body
rumbling day
and night
on the rugged road

toward the sky

The Poor Old Road

dusty and exhausted
the poor old road
keeps pleading for some rest

but the boys
keep laughing and shouting
and drag him down
the hill

A Flower Dropping Its Petals

never
can I listen calmly
to you counting

forget me
forget me not
forget me
forget me not ...

to the last petal

A Snowy Day

The white cat
stretches
and shakes

You little devil
shedding hair
all over the carpet

Evening at Yellowstone

Right after sundown
the animals in hiding
all rush to the edge of the woods
and set their twinkling eyes
in the openings
among the leaves and branches

A beautiful dream design is waiting
waiting for the call of the first star
to soar
into the evening sky

Photograph

The shutter flashes
your instant smile

Then in a mildewed evening
you stare at the yellowed album
and sigh

Happy days are gone

At the Clockshop

Oblivious of time
the clocks on the wall
just keep ticking
busily going
their own
ways

II.

YEAR OF THE HORSE

The Great Wall

1
The struggle between civilization
and barbarism
must be ferocious

See this Great Wall
it twists and turns
with no end in sight

2
What romantic valor
drove us to climb
the ragged ridge
and look long and hard
through a self-adjusting lens
at the skeleton of the dragon
that sprawls miles and miles
in the Waste Time

Yellow River

If you trace up the turbid current
you will find
as any geography book can tell you
the Kunlun Mountains in Qinghai

Yet according to history's bloody accounts
this river
which turns clear at most
once in a thousand years
has its origin in millions of eye sockets
of suffering human beings

Porters on Mount Huangshan

Every step
makes the whole mountain
shake
and tilt

We turn sideways at the edge
of the steep stone steps
to let their heavy burden
and panting breath
press by
then listen to their bent legs
rattling on

Coolie
clog
coolie
clog ...

Photographic Negative

Beating gongs and drums
they celebrate light
in a world
where black
is white

Drinking Tea at a Family Reunion after Thirty Long Years of Separation

Down at one gulp
how unbearable it would have been
to taste drop by drop
the cup of thirty bitter years

You smile and say to me
good tea
should be sipped
and savored

The Tree That Is Shoved Off the Scene

Out of focus
A tree stands in mute amazement
and watches before him
another group of tourists
devouring the scenery
with shiny teeth

Year of the Horse

A dashing horse
is always one step
ahead
of the rolling dust

In the year of the horse
one ought to make
365
hoofbeats

Terraced Paddies

Toiling hard
to build green-carpeted stairs
on a steep slope
for the heaven-ascending gods
to step on

The Night Flute

Let the ever-rising pitch
of the wind
from the bamboo grove
lead
a pair of sleepless eyes
massaging
towards the dark end
of the alley

Years ago in Taiwan
blind masseuses used to roam
the city alleys
playing flutes made of bamboo
in search of customers.

Rainy Season, Taipei

1
restless

in the stuffy
hotel room

a drenched
vacation

2
outside the window
the slanting poles
of rain
are fishing in the cold waves
for the lost
spring

3
once something reminds me
that winter here is cold
and damp
every joint
of my memory
starts aching

The Homesick Drunkard

He has walked a short alley
into a tortuous,
writhing intestine
of ten thousand miles

One step left
ten years
one step right
ten years
O mother
I am struggling
toward
you

III.

IN THE WINDY CITY

Chicago Winter

even steel trembles
so do teeth

red lights burn in turns
at each icy corner
the eyes don't
warm

on two feet
with two hands
pulling down a hat
and tightening the scalp
you greet the wind

Watching Snow

1
As the footprints in the snow
  get deeper and deeper
they become harder and harder
  to comprehend

2
A sudden toll
  of the bell
shakes down
  the snow
from the Cross

Hopscotch

Standing in the way
of a bullet's joyflight
another little girl's blood
stains the pavement

As she falls
a triumphant smile
crosses her twisted face —
finally she managed
to plant both feet
neatly
in the chalked squares

Chicago Serenade

Evening
a desolate street

A car with its windows tightly
rolled up
stops for the red lights

Suddenly
in the rear-view mirror
a dark figure
looming

      Sir, buy ...

The ashen-faced driver
steps on the pedal
and rushes through the red lights
like a rabbit running for its life

      ... buy some flowers
      today's Valentine's Day

Midwest Floods, 1993

Ground Control to
Shuttle Columbia

Backyard flooded
return immediately

New Year Party

at zero hour
they raise their glasses
and sing auld lang syne
bidding farewell
to the old days

then turn around
and shout with joy
while new resolutions
rising
from the bubbling champagne
turn into
colorful balloons
that fill the air

Fashion

Whirling through the revolving door
she finds the fashion she just bought
already out of style

From mini to midi to maxi and
back again
Every year she adjusts her legs
as if they were a tripod (bipod?)

And how a dress shrinks and loses
its shape
once it leaves
the model on display

Every Time I See

Every time I see a little tree
budding timidly
in the spring breeze
I have an urge
to hold your thin shoulder in my arm
and squeeze

Fog

take off your glasses
look the world
nakedly
in the
eye

Floating Flowers

on my front lawn
a swarm of butterflies
is busily dress-rehearsing
a midsummer day's dream

But merrily chasing each other
in mid-air
the two in bright yellow
are in no hurry to come down
and take their places

Today's Sunshine Is So Wonderful

I set up the easel
enthusiastically started my painting

As soon as I finished covering the canvas
    with sky blue
a bird flew into the scene
I said, good, good, you came at the right time
please move up a little. Yes, that's it!
then a green tree rose from the lower
    left corner
just in time to meet a passing white cloud
and the squirrels chasing each other
were not hard to catch
soon I had a presentable painting at hand

Yet I felt something was missing
something deep and inharmonious
to bring out its purity and innocence

As I was busily mixing
some harsh and bleak color
a lonesome old man staggered into
    the picture
and finished my masterwork

Winter Night

When he awakens the ash-covered
passions
with the blow of a pair of tongs
flames lick noisily
at the frozen darkness of the room
and white fog rises before his eyes
like the aroma of milk
in the spring sun

Storm Approaching

A tree
holding up the falling sky
suddenly dropped
its hands
and caught
a
   fleeing
       bird

Chicago

dozing off
in the virgin forest
beneath the feet
of Picasso's strange animal
suddenly a long yell
TIM --- BER ---
awakens me

I raise my head
and in the sunlight that leaks
through
I see the skyscrapers
all slanting towards me

At the Art Institute

1
Please do not touch

Underneath this cool-looking
brassy skin
a sun from the Big Bang
still burns
fiercely

2
A broken arm
of ancient clay
halts the rush hour traffic
for the passing
Time Express

IV.

DIALOGUE

Out of Eden

The snake finds
even a straight way
becomes torturous twists
and turns

pausing from time to time
it raises its head
to hiss at the endless road
to salvation

Dialogue

What are you running away from, old woman?
ARMY
what kind of army? red army or white army?
ARMY

What are you hiding from, young mother?
BOMBS
where are the bombs from? east or west?
BOMBS

What are you crying about, little girl?
BLOOD
whose blood? human or animal?
BLOOD

Croatian Funeral

uninvited mourners
the Serbian shells
wail
from funeral
to funeral
death
after
death

Bosnian Winter

Shielding an old man
from the streaming bullets
the dying tree
watches pityingly
the dying man
chop down
a blackened limb
and drag it
toward another ash-cold
night

Watching the Ocean
in San Francisco
with a Former Red Guard

another wave rushed in
as I was about to ask the question
"Did you think of poetry in those days?"
it crashed on the black rocks
and retreated with a white sigh

we looked away at the bay
through a thick fog
suddenly the sun appeared
brilliant and solemn
as if it were a miracle

but we both knew
it was there all the time

Portrait

They kept enlarging his image
until its every pore
became a great
hollow

But before it could be put
into the big frame of history
Time, the critical old man
already started the work
of reduction
step by step
as he walked backward
squinting at it
from a distance

Picasso Died This Morning

I frittered away the remaining afternoon
and walked up to the window many times
to see if the sky held any last surprise

As it hung over my neighbor's roof
the sun seemed almost
immortal. Picasso died this morning
I don't know what tunes
the three musicians are going to play
I don't know which way
the dove is going to fly

After showing us the world
is still soft and kneadable
the masterly hands are now withdrawing
I reached out unconsciously
but realizing how childish it was
my grasping hands turned to clapping

African Boy

wriggles day and night
a monstrous stomach
in the bloating belly

sucking up
the unblossomed laughter
sucking up
the teardrops
that moisten a mother's heart
sucking up the meager flesh
under his wrinkled skin
sucking up
the indifference in his eyes
and eventually sucking up
from his open mouth a ghastly cry
which we take for soundless
but is in fact at a pitch
well beyond the limit
of our comprehension

Television

the world
is easily
switched off

yet not quite

a spark of hatred
from the dimming screen
suddenly bursts into flames
soon spreading
over Vietnam
over the Middle East
over every feverish face

Extraterrestrials

the evening newscast
is swarming with images
of extraterrestrials

Protruding foreheads
dark and skinny
and big eyes
staring straight out
from sunken sockets

What?
starving Africans?
no wonder they look
so familiar

On the Treacherous Night Sea

a broken refugee boat appears
like a ghost
on the tired sleepless eyelids
jolting and rolling
toward the ever-narrowing harbor
of humanity
toward the shore
where the lights die out
one after another

White House Dream

A night's snow
turns every house
into the White House

Nancy darling
what does the astrologer say on TV
can I go to work
this morning?

Memorial Day

At Arlington, someone
Unknown goes down

The thousands, the thousands
Who have gone down in faraway fields
But who won't die in the heart—
How do we bury
the thousands

Vietnam War Memorial

A block of marble
and twenty six letters of the alphabet
enable history to accommodate
so many young names

Wandering alone
an old woman has at last found
her only child
among the many
and with her eyes tightly shut
she is now feeling for the mortal wound
with her trembling fingers
on his ice-cold forehead

Inflation

A bundle of bills
could buy
a flattering
smile
not long ago

Now
a bundle of bills
can buy
more than
one flattering
smile

Greenhouse

We then drove to the greenhouse
to see if the Cross was in bloom
the Cross that was planted nearly
2000 years ago
the Cross that was once watered
with blood

Still Life 1

the bird and the gun
stare
at each other

just to see
who will be first
to blink

Still Life 2

After a long winter's illness
an emaciated vase
coughs out
a bloody red
rose
in the bright sunshine
of April

Still Life 3

The Goddess of Mercy
of white porcelain
stands there
and watches with a smile
a dust mote fall
in the bright morning light

Growing pains

The branches stretch upward
trying hard to touch the bright sky
while the roots
yearning for warmth, moisture and
darkness
reach for the deep soil

After a sharp pain
of growing, the tree relaxes
as the boy agonizing over
the weighty question
of his being
now laughs and walks away
taller

Performers

The performing monkey
stretches out its hand
like a man
asking the spectators
for money

The performing man
stretches out his hand
like a monkey
asking the monkey
for money

Road

Twisting and turning
yet the road
constantly draws people
forward

It never thinks of itself
as the only right way—
at every crossing
there's always a big sign pointing
TO WHAT TOWN
HOW MANY MILES

Shadow of A Void

The sky becomes dizzy
watching
a circling falcon
train its beak
upon a panic-stricken rabbit

A sharp cry flashes
and is gone
only the shadow of a void remains
dazzling
like a bloody new wound

Under the Night Sky

a wolf
howling at the sky

smells
the bait
inside his fence

drops his tail
and becomes
a dog

Composition

If the sea gulls were not given
a resting place
the sea would surely be lonely

And so the daring boats leave port
and sail
with their high masts

Feet and Hands

Let feet do the task
that hands cannot handle

Carrying the not-big-enough fists
the feet
turn ever so slowly
and suddenly
dart

Foot and Shoe

A blistered foot
squirms
seeking compromise
from the shoe

Drum Beats

A hairy fist
bangs relentlessly
on a civilized chest
that tries in vain
to make some flimsy
arguments

Old Woman

like a worn-out record
the deep grooves
on her forehead
repeat and repeat

I want to live
I want to live
I want to

V.

FOUR SEASONS

Spring's First Dandelion

It most likely was blown here
last fall, from some faraway place
an immigrant of a sort
yet it now produces
the year's first surprise

After a long winter
in the earth
that embraces all and nurtures all
a yellow flower emerges
and thus begins
a new spring

Spring Thunder

Waking me up
in the middle of the night
just to tell me
of his rumbling heart

Spring

Spring is a bed
sweet
yet short

Just as you are about to yawn
after awaking from hibernation
you find your outstretched limbs
abruptly confined

Rainy Season

Over and over
repeating always the same old stuff

drip drip drip
chip chip chip

O how desperately we long for
a deafening thunder
or an overwhelming shout

SHUT UP

Typhoon Season

Every year at this time
the woman within me
rages violently
with no provocation

And when it's over
I always hear her
licking my bleeding heart
with her tender tongue

Autumn

a busy season
so many dreams
to sweep up

suddenly she rises
and says
it's time to go
then turns
and leaves

Autumn Tree

Upon the arrival of autumn
a tree
suddenly becomes scared
stretching desperately its shadow
to cover more ground

Under its feet
crises mushroom
and flourish

Autumn Leaves

Every leaf
helps
thicken
the carpet
&
soften

    •

    •

    •

  the

    •

    •

  fall

Autumn Window

Now that she is middle-aged, my wife
likes to stand before the window
and comb her hair

Her only makeup a trace of cloud
the landscape of a graceful
poised maturity

Four Seasons

Spring

Only the survivors of the deep snow
can open up
their most delicate and colorful
inner selves
to the world
without hesitation

Summer

To the scorched earth
we offer our humble sweat

These sparkling dewdrops
coming from the sea of life
have a salty taste

Autumn

When his wife and children
comb and find a grey hair
on his head
he can detect an unsuppressible joy
of the gleaners
in their exclamations

Winter

The colder the day is
the brighter the furnace burns

There is no energy crisis
in our hearts

Birds * Four Seasons

Spring

If you wish to know
the shortest distance
between two trees
on this bright, enchanting day
any of the small, swift birds
can tell you with their twitter

It's not a straight line

Summer

At noon
struck by a flaming light
a small bird
plummets through
dense leafy shade

Until slowly awakening
to discover himself
standing on a tree
lush and luxuriant

All that can be green
is green

Autumn

When did the eyes
become so blurry

A bird flying higher and higher
discovered
its own reflection in a pond
the smaller the clearer

Winter

The last thread of mist
drifting in the air
finally joins
the icicles beneath the eaves

In this weather
how can I criticize
a small bird's song
brief and evasive

Trees * Four Seasons

Spring

Bury the wrinkles of time
deep in the bottom of your heart

Every time I see you
you're as young as ever

Summer

Lofty season

A thick-plumed bird
on a branch
looks about perkily

Just as it should be, green,
everything green

Autumn

Loud and clear
is it a screech of an insect
frightened at the sudden solitude
or a ringing in the hollow ears
after the noisy festival?

Winter

When he grasps
there's nothing left
but the last leaf

In a howling north wind
an old man
laughing bitterly, releases the leaf
and mutters
go, go, all of you go
fly high and go far away

If You Are ...

If you are an umbrella
please save the last pure ray of the sun
wait until the next spring wakens
I will release a heaven full of magnificence

If you are a kite
remember your place in the sky
wait until the next spring wakens
Tell me then, of the child that held the string,
how much taller he has grown

If you are a flower
please lift slowly your humble head
wait until the next spring wakens
I can say, " You haven't changed a bit"

If you are a window
lower your curtain
wait until the next spring wakens
I will astonish you with a little mystery, joy

If you are a poet
please warm a kettle of wine of a thousand years
wait until the next spring wakens
I will come and collect your new poems,
     sweet and aromatic

If you are a waterfall
let me gently roll you up
wait until the next spring wakens
I will show you a vista of mountains and waters
     painted in calligrapher's ink

If you are the sound of drums
follow the breeze into every sorrowful heart
wait until the next spring wakens
I will come and collect from one and all,
     an earth shattering sound of early thunder

If you are a tear
hold on, disappear from the face of the strong
wait until the next spring wakens
Come then, decorate beneath the happy eyes,
     a feast of furious rain

William Marr, born in China in 1936, came to the United States in 1961 as a graduate engineering student and is now a researcher at Argonne National Laboratory outside of Chicago. Under the pseudonym Fei Ma, he is the author of nine volumes of poetry, all written in his native language. He has translated the works of many contemporary American and European poets into Chinese. Some of his own poems have been translated into Japanese, Korean and Slavic and have been included in several English anthologies. He has received many honors, including three awards from Taiwan for his poetry and translations. He is the editor of *Forty Modern Poets of Taiwan*, *Modern Poetry in Taiwan* and *Anthology of Contemporary Chinese Poetry*, published in China, Hong Kong, and Taiwan, respectively. From 1993 to 1995, he served as president of the Illinois State Poetry Society.

Some comments on the author's previous works:

He uses fluently and clearly the language of the common people.... gives profound meaning to common objects and events.

--- Dominic Cheung, editor
The Isle Full of Noises
Modern Chinese Poetry from Taiwan
Columbia University Press

Unquestionably among the best contemporary Chinese poets....he is unique and without peer in the arena of short poems.

--- Ray Y.W. Lau
Huaxia Poetry
Guangzhou, China

His concise yet highly symbolic poetry, with a deep sense of humanity, adds a new dimension to the rich tradition of Chinese poetry....he bridges the gap between new and old, and between East and West.

--- Ji-Tang Gu
Hong Kong Literature Monthly